COMPANION TO
SAINT PETER

by
J.B. Midgley

*All booklets are published thanks to the
generous support of the members of the
Catholic Truth Society*

CATHOLIC TRUTH SOCIETY
PUBLISHERS TO THE HOLY SEE

CONTENTS

Introduction 3

Devotion to Saint Peter 6

The First Disciples 15

The Foundation of the Church 25

Holy Thursday 40

The Primacy of Peter 53

Acknowledgements 72

Introduction

Pope John Paul II recently reminded the Church that Christ, the Eternal Good Shepherd, appointed Peter to be the chief shepherd of His Flock so that His loving care should be experienced in time and that salvation should reach to the ends of the earth. In the exercise of this pastoral office which he and the Bishops have inherited, he welcomes the dawn of a new millenium as an opportunity to proclaim the good news of God's Kingdom with renewed confidence.

St Peter, Prince of the Apostles, has bequeathed to us his divinely inspired profession of faith which is the Rock upon which Christ built His Church. As guardian of the keys to Heaven's gates, Peter continues to guide us in the challenges of successive ages. He has left the memory of a life characterised by an absolute commitment born of love for Jesus, and an heroic witness which is an inspiration and reassurance of faith. It is hoped that these pages may contibute towards renewed appreciation of a Saint in whose abiding friendship we always find eager and powerful support.

J.B. Midgley,
Downham Market, Lent 2003.

The Life of St Peter

Simon, son of Jonah, came from Bethsaida on the shores of the Sea of Galilee where he was head of the family fishing consortium. When his brother Andrew became a disciple of Jesus, he introduced Simon to the Lord who immediately re-named him 'Cephas' (Peter) which means 'Rock' and describes the stability and reliability which serves the Church so well. He was the first to proclaim Christ's divinity as the Son of the living God and, with James and John, witnessed His Transfiguration. The same trio was present when Our Lord restored Jairus' daughter to life, and they accompanied Him to the Garden of Gethsamane on the night before He died. As long as Peter was with Jesus, he was confident loyal, generous and warmhearted, but he fell asleep when his Master most needed the solace of companionship, denied knowing Him three times and, like us, could be impetuous, uncertain and frightened. In an act of loving reconciliation which obliterated the triple denial and the results of human frailty, the Risen Lord made sure that Peter was the first Apostle to whom he appeared, and before He ascended to His Father He entrusted him with the care of His Flock.

Peter's leadership and decision making qualities quickly became apparent when he arranged the election of Judas' replacement, preached with outstanding courage and success after receiving the gifts of the Holy Spirit at

Pentecost, competently defended the Apostles' position before a hostile Sanhedrin, and insisted on fidelity to the principle of the early Church that all things should be shared in common. Hesitation and fear were no more as he bravely endured an unjust imprisonment which could have culminated in execution, made the problematic decision to recognise the right of Gentiles to become Christians, undertook hazardous missionary journeys and, with Paul, nurtured the Church in Rome. The names "first Pope" and "Bishop of Rome" illuminate Peter's incomparable vocation, and his establishment of the episcopal continuity which exists to this day. Clement, Ignatius of Antioch, and Irenaeus all testify to the efficacy of his purposeful leadership in Rome, the 'Babylon' where he wrote his First Epistle, and to his shining martyrdom at the hands of Nero in 64 AD.

DEVOTION TO SAINT PETER

Peter inspired great affection because, in the vivid characterisation drawn by the New Testament, we catch a glimpse of his own failings and aspirations. He was quick-tempered, impulsive, selfish, generous, brave, frightened, striving to go forward, and often retreating. In the end, however, he was the great leader who vindicated Jesus' choice, a bold and eloquent preacher of God's Kingdom, His Fatherhood and the brotherhood of man. His heroism and nobility shone forth and he died defending the Faith, a willing martyr for the beloved Lord whose teachings he upheld. His life is a testament to the truth of Christianity and, even from his hesitancy in fully appreciating the immensity of Jesus' message, we learn that God's power and love never wavers.

Greek and Latin graffiti in the catacombs of the third century illustrate the veneration in which Peter was held, both in the earliest liturgies and in private devotion. He has been invoked as a saint for the whole world, the guardian of Heaven's gates, and the ever accessible and powerful patron of Church and Papacy. In England, the Abbeys of Canterbury, Glastonbury, Malmesbury, Peterborough, Lindisfarne, Whitby, Westminster; and the cathedrals of York, Lichfield, Worcester and Selsby are dedicated to him, as is Peterhouse, Cambridge University's first college. Before the Reformation eleven hundred churches bore his name, and another three hundred honoured him in partnership with Saint Paul. Today, with the Most Blessed Virgin, St Joseph and St Edward, he is patron of Westminster, the mother-diocese of English and Welsh Catholics.

Artistic impressions of Peter are generally consistent. He is of solid build, has an authoritative but benevolent countenance framed by grey hair and a short square beard, though some artists have given him a bald or tonsured head. He is pictured with a ship which represents the Church, the "Barque of Peter" on an even keel giving safe passage to all. Sometimes he has a fish, a reminder of his occupation and appointment as a "fisher of men", or a cockerel reminiscent of the night he denied Jesus, or holding a set of the keys given to him as gatekeeper of the Kingdom of Heaven. He wears a toga or episcopal vestments, and may be crowned with a papal tiara. Origen, and later Eusebius, wrote that when Peter was condemned to crucifixion he asked if it might be head downwards because he did not consider himself worthy to die in the same position as his Master. His martyrdom is honoured, therefore, in images of his inverted crucifixion. In England he appears in screen paintings, sculptures and stained-glass windows and, since the Norman Conquest, he has given a popular

Christian name to boys and, in its Greek form, to girls. The Brancacci family chapel of the Carmine church in Florence houses Masaccio's frescoes of the events of Saint Peter's life recorded in the Gospel and Acts of the Apostles, the continued significance of which is the subject of the following pages.

The Liturgy

Rome was a meeting place for various nationalities and creeds from all over the Empire and at first Jewish Christians practised the faith in relative safety, though there were dangerous periods, as when Caligula temporarily expelled the Jews mainly because the Romans were jealous of Jewish commercial success. Peter had been at the centre of key events during Jesus' life on earth, and was commissioned by Him to be the chief pastor. Some say he went to assume leadership in Rome as early as 42AD after Caligula's death and was certainly supporting the community with Paul about 60AD. The reign of Nero saw a resumption of persecution which culminated in 64AD when the city was destroyed by a fire probably ordered by the emperor who blamed the Christians. Peter, we know, was crucified but Paul, who had been born in Tarsus, was decapitated in accord with the dignity of a Roman citizen. From her earliest days, the Church has commemorated their martyrdom on June 29th, a date which suggests they died

Devotion to Saint Peter

on the festival of Romulus at the Circus of Gaius, a few hundred yards from the present Vatican. On this day, the two princes of the Apostles share the Vigil and Solemnity in the Roman Calendar.

The reading from the Acts of the Apostles records that Peter performed the first Apostolic miracle. He and John were entering the Temple for the prayers which were said at the ninth hour when a man, lame from birth, was being carried to the Beautiful Gate where the destitute traditionally begged alms from the worshippers. When he asked them for help Peter said, "'I have neither silver nor gold, but I will give you what I have: in the name of Jesus Christ the Nazarene, walk!' Peter then took him by the hand and helped him to stand up. Instantly, his feet and ankles became firm, he jumped up, stood, and began to walk, and he went with them into the Temple, walking and jumping and praising God." Peter knew that by invoking the authority of Jesus Christ he would attract the hostility of the Temple priesthood who would see it as an affront to their authority, but he did not hesitate to act on behalf of the compassionate God. The Office of Readings for the Solemnity St Augustine says, "It was logical for the Lord to entrust the care of the sheep to Peter after his Resurrection. He was not, of course, the only disciple worthy of this responsibility. When Christ spoke to one, all were included: Peter was addressed first because he was the foremost Apostle." (*Sermon* 295; *Ac* 3:1-10)

The Intercessions of the Liturgy of the Hours provide a beautiful prayer which is always relevant. "We pray to Christ who built his Church on the foundation of the Apostles and the Prophets. Lord, you called Simon the fisherman to be a fisher of men; call others to share in his task. When the disciples feared the ship was sinking, you commanded the sea and there was calm; protect your Church in the midst of trouble, and give her the peace that the world cannot give. After your Resurrection, you gathered your Church around Peter; gather all your people into the unity for which you prayed, and let your good news be preached through all creation. You entrusted the keys of your kingdom to your Church; open the gates of life to the departed souls who put their trust in you." (Adapted).

Other Feasts of St Peter

Three other Feasts of Saint Peter once adorned the Roman Calendar and are worth remembering in the context of Church history, Peter's primacy, and the devotion of earlier generations.

January 18th: "Saint Peter's Chair in Rome" celebrates the episcopal See of Rome as the centre of the Universal Church and seat of the Supreme Pontiffs who are Peter's successors. The Octave of Prayer for Christian Unity begins on this day and ends on January 25th, the Feast of the Conversion of Saint Paul. It includes the invocations "That they all may be one as thou Father in me and I in

Devotion to Saint Peter

Thee; that the world may believe that Thou hast sent me." "And I say unto thee, thou art Peter and upon this rock I will build my Church; and the gates of hell will not prevail against it, and to thee I will give the keys of the Kingdom of Heaven." (*Jn* 17:21; *Mt* 16:18-19)

February 22nd: "St Peter's Chair at Antioch" commemorates his authoritative Gospel mission to the Gentiles, and the fruitful establishment of the first Gentile Church in Antioch where the followers of Jesus were first described as Christians.

August 1st: "Saint Peter Ad Vincula" celebrates his miraculous escape from prison and certain death thanks to the intervention of an Angel sent by God.

A synthesis of related prayers from the Roman Missal of 1949, is here translated and adapted as reverently as possible. "Lord, you gave your blessed Apostle Peter the keys of the heavenly kingdom and the papal authority to bind and to loose. Grant that, through his intercession, we may be released from the chains of our sins, and that the prayers and offerings of your Church will secure our pardon. Just as you delivered him unharmed from his prison chains, we ask you to free us from the bonds of our sins and to protect us from every evil. May the holy sacrifice of the Mass which we offer to you win us new life and, with Peter's watchful care, may no storm overwhelm us whom you have made safe on the rock of apostolic teaching and tradition."

Hymns and prayers in honour of Saint Peter

"Wouldst thou a patron see thy cause defending?
Christ's Chief Apostle be all thy befriending.
Thou didst thy Master grieve, yet pardon borrow;
May we our faults retrieve with daily sorrow.

As once an angel freed the chains that bound thee,
Loose thou the souls in need thou seest around thee.
Firm rock, our Saviour saith, pillar unyielding,
Strengthen the Church, her faith from error shielding.

Let not the tempter's snare our feet entangle,
Nor wolves presumptuous dare thy flock to mangle.
In death's tremendous hour on thee relying,
His rage we'll overpower, valiant in dying.
Key-bearer, we implore, grace by thy prayers restore;
Grant us through heaven's door entrance hereafter."

(*'Si vis patronum quaerere'*, 18th Century, Tr R.A. Knox)

DEVOTION TO SAINT PETER

"Peter, we salute you. We thank you for your witness and join with you in praising our glorious Lord and Saviour. Like you, may we joyfully anticipate His second coming as we work for his Kingdom to be established now wnd forever." *(St Augustine.)*

"All powerful Father, you have built your Church on the rock of Saint Peter's confession of faith. May nothing divide or weaken our unity in faith and love." *(Opening Prayer, Feast of The Chair of Saint Peter Apostle, February 22nd since the re-ordering of the Roman Calendar, 1969-70.)*

"O surely he was blest with blessedness unpriced,
Who, taught of God, confessed the Godhead in the Christ;
For of thy Church Lord, thou didst own thy saint a true
  foundation-stone.
Thrice fallen, thrice restored; the bitter lesson learnt,
That heart for thee O Lord with triple ardour burnt;
The cross he took he laid not down until he grasped the
  martyr's crown."
(Bishop W.Walsham How, 1823-97.)

Prayers for the Pope

"Almighty and eternal God, have mercy on your servant John Paul our Pope and direct him according to your clemency into the way of everlasting salvation; that he may desire by your grace those things that are agreeable to you, and perform them with all his strength. Through Christ Our Lord, Amen." (*'A Simple Prayer Book, Catholic Truth Society, 1986.*)

"Behold O kind and most sweet Jesus, I cast myself down on my knees in thy sight and with themost fervent desire of my soul I pray and beseech thee that thou wouldst impress upon my heart lively sentiments of Faith, Hope and Charity, with true repentance for my sins and a firm desire for amendment; whilst with deep affection and grief of soul I ponder within myself and mentally contemplate thy five most precious wounds, having before my eyes that which David spoke in prophecy of thee O my good Jesus, 'They have pierced my hands and my feet; they have numbered all my bones'."

"Let us pray for our Holy Father, the Pope: The Lord preserve him, give him life, make him blessed upon the earth, and deliver him not to the will of his enemies."

Our Father... Hail Mary... Glory be to the Father...
(Preces et Pia Opera, 171.)

THE FIRST DISCIPLES

Palestine

The land of Canaan which God promised to the descendants of Abraham, lies between the Mediterranean and the Jordan, and extends from Lebanon in the north to the Egyptian desert in the south. After the Philistines arrived from Crete in 11th century BC, it became known as Palestine, a territory of one hundred and fifty miles from Mount Hermon in the north to the Dead Sea in the south, and fifty separating the western coastal plains from the desert in the east. The River Jordan runs through valleys bordered by green pastures and fertile fields on one side, and by the barren uplands of Judaea and Samaria on the other. From a central position in the ancient world, it linked the civilisations of Europe and Mesopotamia, and was a focus for trade and philosophy in established and developing societies. This relatively prosperous province of the Empire harvested sufficient wheat, barley, olives, dates, grapes and figs to provide a surplus for export. Sheep and goats were adequately pastured, and the forests yielded as much timber as was needed.

After the Exodus, 'Israel' became the collective name of the twelve tribes descended from the twelve sons of Jacob, and synonymous with the Jewish nation. When Joshua apportioned the Promised Land, the sons of Zebulun, Issachar, and Asher received Galilee which extended from the rugged northern hills, through the uplands bordering the Plain of Genesereth and the Valley of Esdraelon, to the central hill country of Bethshan. The Sea of Galilee, variously called the Lake of Galilee, Lake Tiberias, and the Sea of Genesereth, is thirteen miles long and seven wide. In Jesus' day, it gave a livelihood to the fishing communities whose catches were salted at the lake-side town of Tarichaea, 'Pickling Factory', and eaten throughout Palestine. City dwellers in the south tended to be scornful of their rural neighbours, which is somewhat ironic in that Galilee surpassed Jerusalem in national pride and resistance to foreign rule. The upper-class in Jerusalem knew that its continued affluence depended on political and economic stability, so it cultivated ostensibly good relationships with government, whether it was that of Herod or a Roman procurator. To some extent this explains why the Gospels contrast the enthusiasm of Galileans for the Messianic Kingdom with the indifference of Jerusalem's inhabitants which caused Jesus to weep over their city.

The town of Bethsaida ("the house of fishing"), built by the tribe of Nephthali, and developed by Herod Antipas, is on the north-west shore of the Sea of Galilee. Jesus knew it well, taught in the synagogue, and worked miracles there, though He had to take the residents to task for being unmoved by the evidence he gave about the Kingdom.

Jonah, a fisherman, lived there with his two sons Simon and Andrew. The Fathers of the Church are not certain which brother was the elder, but agree that it was Simon who directed a fishing co-operative, members of which included James and John, the sons of Zebedee and, probably, Thomas, and Nathanael who is later called Batholomew. The group owned one of the sturdy, expensive vessels which fished the waters, and employed casual labour for its maintenance and the servicing of nets and sails. No doubt the management experience developed Simon's leadership skills which Jesus recognised and put to noble use. (cf. *Lk* 10:13-16; *Jn* 21:1-2).

John the Baptist's cleansing ritual of baptism in the Jordan had evoked precious memories of the Hebrews' liberation from Egyptian slavery, and their escape through the Red Sea on their way to the Promised land of Canaan. Simon, Andrew, James and John were among the many drawn to his teaching about God's universal reign, and salvation through repentance and reconciliation. Now that the Messiah had, at last, arrived, John knew that his mission as last prophet and herald was complete and that he must relinquish the discipleship of his followers in favour of One whose eminence must grow as his diminished. Andrew and John were there when he identified Jesus as "the Lamb of God who takes away the sins of the world", and were immediately attracted. They declared their wish to be His disciples by addressing Him as "Rabbi" and, such was the impact of this meeting that they remembered ever after the time of their new allegiance. "It was about the tenth hour", 4.00pm our time, when He took them to His lodgings in Bethania where they spent the remainder of a happy day with Him, and stayed overnight as eastern hospitality recommended.

Next morning, Andrew rushed to tell Simon the wonderful news that they had found the Messiah, the anointed King of Israel who had been expected for four thousand years. He wanted his brother to benefit from an early introduction, especially if there was the possibility of preferment in the new kingdom. Simon made no protest of disbelief as they went to Jesus who, with a sign of divine omniscience, greeted him by name, even adding that of his father: "You are Simon, son of Jonah." Then, with the first intimation of the Church's foundation, He "Christened" him with the Aramaic name "Cephas", in Greek "Petros", meaning "Rock". It would take some time for the rock-like qualities to become fully apparent but, with God's grace, Peter would become an inspiring leader, an impassioned teacher, and authoritative writer. In St Paul's words, we are all "part of a building that has the apostles and the prophets for its foundation, and Christ Jesus Himself for its main corner-stone. As every structure is aligned on Him, all grow into one holy temple in the Lord...built into a house where God lives in the Spirit." (cf. *Jn* 1:28; 21:15-19; *1 Co* 15:5; *Ep* 2:20).

Capernaum

An inconspicuous fishing settlement a few miles west of Bethsaida became the first significant place reached as one crossed the Jordan frontier from the east. It was developed as as military port and provincial seat of Roman government, with a garrison commanded by a centurion whose main task was to ensure the collection of taxes, especially the lucrative toll-charges and revenues from the fishing industry. These were a great burden on the people, especially when Herod Antipas wanted extra funds to build his capital at Tiberias and the fortress palace of Machaerus where John the Baptist was killed. The future St Matthew was a tax-collector for the area and one of the "publicans" despised by the Jews for their co-operation with the occupying power, and regarded as sinners who were contaminated by their continued association with Gentiles.

Capernaum was a convenient rendezvous for pilgrims joining caravans going to Jerusalem for the Paschal and other Feasts. It also benefited from the trade routes connecting Egypt to Mesopotamia, Damascus, Arabia, and Gaza which followed a north-easterly direction through Galilee. Because they were thus by-passed, the Judaeans hardened in their insularity and suspected that the Galileans were half-heathen. The town memorably figures in the lives of Our Lord and Peter who moved to his wife's birthplace shortly after their wedding, and

Andrew followed soon after. Jesus was a regular visitor and was so fond of Capernaum that it became like a second home. There He taught in the synagogue, promised the Eucharist, and healed many people including Peter's mother-in-law whose recovery was so instant that she rose from her sick-bed and made them all a meal. Little is known of Peter's wife other than that she probably belonged to the group of loyal women who followed Jesus, and that she courageously accompanied her husband on missionary journeys which were fraught with hardship and danger. (cf. *Mt* 8:14-15; *1 Co* 9:15).

Jesus defines the mission of Peter and his colleagues.

Peter, James, John, and the other disciples went regularly to learn from their new Master while continuing to earn their living in the fishing consortium. Towards the end of the first year of His public life, Jesus was with them one morning at the lake-side as they were sorting out their nets. They had been fishing all night, generally considered to be the most favourable time, but had caught nothing. Though they had witnessed His miracle at the wedding in Cana, it says much about the trusting relationship which had been established that expert fishermen took a Carpenter's advice when He told them to try again. The reward of a huge catch moved Peter to fall to his knees and beg, "Leave me Lord; I am a sinful man."

THE FIRST DISCIPLES

The plea is reminiscent of Isaiah's reaction when God asked him to be His messenger to the people. He was burdened with a sense of unworthiness in the face of God's holiness, and Peter felt the same. He had fished at the right time and achieved nothing; Jesus told him to fish at the wrong time and the result was marvellous. Fishermen were bound to be impressed by such a miracle and, to the Semitic mind, such command over the sea and its inhabitants was an indication of divine power. When he confessed his sinfulness, Peter unconsciously acknowledged that when Jesus cured the sick and controlled nature, He demonstrated His mission to cast out sin and establish God's reign in the souls of human beings who are all called to holiness. "Do not be afraid," Jesus said. "From now on it is men you will catch". It was a general invitation but it was Peter to whom He spoke directly. The fisher-disciples beached their boat and left everything to follow Jesus in that instant change of heart with which the attainment of God's Kingdom begins. Whether catching fish or men, His plans do not coincide with human perceptions, and the Apostles gradually learned that a trusting surrender to His will achieves what is beyond unaided human nature. (cf. *Lk* 5:1-11; *Jn2:1*).

The Twelve

Jesus' teaching and miracles attracted such a large following that He decided to appoint a cabinet of twelve leaders. As always, when faced with a momentous decision, He went into the hills and spent the whole night in prayer to God. In the morning, "He summoned His disciples and selected twelve whom He called Apostles: Simon, to whom He gave the name Peter, his brother Andrew, James, John, Philip, Bartholomew (formerly Nathanael), Matthew, Thomas, James the son of Alphaeus, Simon the Zealot (zealous Cananaean), Jude the brother of James, and Judas Iscariot who became a traitor", and whose place would be taken by Matthias. (*Lk* 6: 12-16).

Israelites believed they were descended from Jacob's twelve sons, so in the number of twelve Apostles they saw a revival of Jacob's fortunes in a restored Israel. The Book of Revelation reflects on their twelve patriarchs and the twelve guardians of the shrine whose "walls had twelve gates, and over them were written the names of the twelve tribes of Israel. The walls stood on twelve foundations stones, each of which bore the name of one of the Apostles of the Lamb." It also describes the vision of God's Bride and her role in salvation history. Mary is mother to all God's people, the figure the Church, and Queen of the twelve Apostles whom her Son appointed to preach the good news of the Kingdom which is to come. Their evangelising mission, and that of their successors, is the activity of the Church which Christ established as the sacrament of all God's people from Adam to the end of time. She is the high-walled holy City, the new Jerusalem whose twelve gates open to reveal God's loving intentions from the time when He first called Abraham until the Son's second coming in glory to present to the Father the plan of salvation concluded in the perfected Kingdom . (*Rv* 12:1; 21:9-14; cf. *Liturgy of the Assumption of the Blessed Virgin Mary,* August 15th).

Except for Matthew, the Twelve were not drawn from the ranks of the wealthy, the powerful, or the religious professionals, but their experience, capacity for hard work, and familiarity with the Scriptures which they had studied in the synagogue schools should not be underestimated. They were bi-lingual in Aramaic and Greek, and most had benefited from the teaching of John the Baptist. However, that said, they did not seem a group likely to transform the world in a short space of time. They would profess undying loyalty to their Master, but would be unstable in a crisis, cowardly in their desertion, denial, and treachery. Even when Our Lord's time with them was coming to an end, they habitually misunderstood His teachings, causing Him to reproach them for their clouded perception and lack of faith. Nevertheless, grace triumphs, they vindicate His choice as they reach absolute faith in the Son of God who is the King of Israel.

The shortcomings and diversity of a group which included a former tax-collector loathed for extortion and collaboration with the Romans, illustrate the all-embracing nature of God's Kingdom. His care reaches beyond the confines of race and nation to all whom He has created, even to those who may not yet believe in Him, but whom He includes among the channels of His grace and the ministers of His blessings. Disciples in every age learn from the Apostles to follow Jesus not only when it is convenient and agreeable, but also through the vicissitudes and trials of life. They will face unlikely and demanding choices, but they need not be deterred by a sense of unworthiness or incapacity because divine grace makes possible that which is beyond human accomplishment. Like the Twelve they can rely on personal and community prayer, and as they respond to the gifts of the Holy Spirit in Baptism and Confirmation, they continue Jesus' mission convinced that God always gives strength for the attainment of what He wants done. (cf. *Ac* 1:12-14)

The Foundation of the Church

Peter's profession of faith

In Bethsaida, Jesus restored sight to a blind man, and then went with the Apostles to preach the good news of the Kingdom to the villages around Caesarea Philippi the city near Mount Hermon, about twenty miles north of the Sea of Galilee. Three hundred years earlier, Greek immigrants had built it on the site of a sanctuary in honour of Pan, the deity of shepherds and their flocks, an appropriate foreshadowing of the emerging apostolate, and called it Paneas. When Philip the Tetrarch, a son of Herod the Great, restored and enlarged it, he dedicated the project to Tiberius Caesar, and added his own name. This distinguished it from Caesarea 'Maritima', the Mediterranean city-port built by Herod to ingratiate himself with Augustus, which was the central depot for garrisoned Roman militia, and headquarters of Pontius Pilate when he became Governor of Judaea with Samaria and Idumaea in 26AD.

When news of Jesus' activity reached the court of Herod Antipas, rumours began to circulate that the murdered John the Baptist had come back to life, much to the discomfort of the superstitious ruler. There was a general sense of imminent Messianic arrival with which a return of the prophets was associated, but no one, not even the professional religious leaders like the Scribes and Pharisees, had any idea who it should be, though everyone was intrigued by the carpenter from Nazareth who taught with such authority and miraculously cured the sick. Jesus had not wanted people to get carried away by bursts of Messianic enthusiasm, to misunderstand His message of the Kingdom, or profess belief just because they saw signs and wonders. He had avoided attention and told His followers to keep things to themselves but now, in this place dedicated to pagan worship and political influence, He decided to discuss his own identity and authority. He asked the disciples what the people thought, but they commented only on the speculation about John the Baptist, Elijah himself, or some other prophet like one of those who regularly introduced themselves to society. They said those who thought He might have been the Messiah were disappointed when He did not live up to their expectations of a conquering hero.

To take His Gospel to the whole world, Jesus had selected a special band of Apostles who had seen His miracles, been given authority over unclean spirits, and power to cure disease and sickness. Now, when He asked for their own opinion, He was entitled to expect more than their silent bemusement. Only Peter, with characteristic spontaneity, made a decisive and immediate acknowledgement of his Master as the Messiah: ""You are the Christ, the Son of the Living God." (cf. *Mt* 10:1-7; *Lk* 6:12-16).

The Foundation of the Church

Son of God

In the Old Testament Job saw the angels, "the sons of God", chanting praise to the Creator as they rejoiced in the harmony of creation over which humankind was destined to have mastery. The title is also given to the children of Israel and their rulers, the royal shepherds who represent the tender and intimate care which God has for all His children. The distinction between these "sons of God" and the sublime title which belongs only to the Second Person of the Blessed Trinity, is apparent when the Father says, "It is He who will build a house for me and I will make His throne firm forever. I will be like a Father to Him and He a Son to me."

The Son is the Word who participates in the Creation and continues His creative activity, shaping us to His own likeness and "making us a new creation in Him." In the New Covenant, the Father re-affirms this relationship when Jesus was baptised by John in the Jordan. As He came out of the water, the clouds of Heaven parted and the Spirit, like a dove, descended on Him. "And a voice came from Heaven. You are my Son, the Beloved".This is the revelation of the power and authority of Our Lord who upholds the universe by His word and reflects the glory and accessibility of the Father. In Peter's words, "Jesus Christ is Lord of all men... God anointed Him with the Holy Spirit and with power and, because God was with Him, Jesus went about doing good and curing all who had fallen into the power of the devil." The Father most fully reveals Himself in the Son in whose baptised humanity, we are all born again of water and the Holy Spirit.

When Peter recognised the divine nature of the Son of God who had adopted human nature, Jesus told him that unaided human reason could not have reached such a conclusion, but he was absolutely right because he had been the privileged recipient of a revelation from "my Father in Heaven", the possessive adjective emphasising the unique, divine Sonship. Then He repeated the name He had given him at their first meeting: "You are Peter, and on this rock I will build my Church" which means "the assembly which belongs to the Lord", the House He would build for His Father. He knew Peter would falter from time to time, and even deny knowing Him, but the grace which makes good human weakness would always be there to advance the Father's plan. The early Church believed that it was God the Son who, disguised as an angel, shepherded the Israelites through the wilderness, and quenched their thirst with water from the material rock, in the same way as His blood flows for the world's salvation. The divine primary Founder and Spiritual Rock rewarded Peter's insight with the honour of being the secondary rock, the Church's foundation in Christ who is the Corner Stone of the House of God's Kingdom. One day, Peter would say of his Lord "This is the Stone...which has proved to be the Keystone. For of all the names in the world given to men, this is the only one by which we can be saved." (cf. *Ex* 17:6; 23:20-23; *Nb* 22:11; *Ws* 18:14-15; *1 Co* 10:4; *2 Co* 5:17; *Heb* 1:3; *Ac* 4:11; 10:34-38).

Divine Authority delegated

Christ the Corner Stone promised Peter that the assaults levelled by the "gates of hell" against His Church would not prevail, and the Citadel built on the Rock would never succumb to forces hostile to the cause of good. In the Old Covenant Eliakim, chief minister and steward to King Hezekiah, held the keys of the House of David. In the new dispensation, Our Lord who is both God and Man now gives His Chancellor the keys of the Kingdom which He inaugurates on earth in His Body, the Church. Then He developed the 'rock' metaphor describing the specific powers invested in the primacy of Peter, and the holders of the keys who come after him. "Whatever you bind on earth shall be bound in Heaven, and whatever you loose on earth shall be loosed in Heaven." 'Binding' and 'loosing' are rabbinical expressions of 'exclusion from' or 'admission to' the community or, in the words of the law, a 'prevention' or 'permission'. Jesus, "the one who sanctifies is of the same stock as those he sanctifies" (*Heb* 2:11). The power He delegates to Peter and his successors to promote the cause of the Kingdom, and its rule of love in human hearts, is a divine power. It is this which is exercised in the spiritual order on earth, and concerning which Our Lord will say more to Peter after the Resurrection.

Though the keys betokened leadership of the Apostolic College, Peter consulted the other Apostles. For example, he went to Samaria at their behest because they thought the time had come for the people to hear God's word, and there is much evidence of his close co-operation with Saint John. Yet always he is the Fisherman in charge, the shepherd, the elder of elders with privileged perceptions to correct misunderstandings. God is never bound by Peter and his successors, but what they declare to be of faith is in accord with His will and has permanent validity. "The power to bind and to loose connotes the authority to absolve sins, to pronounce doctrinal judgements, and to make disciplinary decisions in the Church. Jesus entrusted this authority to the Church through the ministry of the Apostles and, in particular, through the ministry of Peter, the only one to whom He specifically entrusted the keys of the Kingdom." (*Catechism of the Catholic Church,* 553; cf. *2 K* 18; *Mt* 16:13-20; *Lk* 5:10; *Jn* 21:1-14; *Ac* 1:9-16; 3:1-11; 4:1-22; 8:14; *2 P* 3:15-16; *Is* 22:22).

The Passion Prophecy

With His Church established and its leader appointed, the moment had come for Jesus to prepare the Apostles about His forthcoming suffering and death in Jerusalem at the hands of the religious leaders. They were shocked

The Foundation of the Church

beyond belief at what he told them. If Peter was right to hail Him as the Son of God and Messiah, how could Israel, the Chosen People, in the persons of the Sanhedrin, reject and kill the One for whom they had been waiting. They found no comfort in His prediction of a resurrection which sounded vague, remote and impossible. The news was particularly overwhelming for Peter who had been first to recognise the fullness of Jesus' identity. Distraught at the thought of losing his Master and Saviour, he tried to be helpful and drew Jesus to one side. "Heaven preserve you Lord," he whispered. "This must not happen to you." Like the rest, he still had hopes of a Messianic triumph which would bring a reign of religious and political prosperity to a restored Kingdom of David.

Jesus' rebuke to Peter "Get behind me Satan", seems harsh because we cannot hear the tone of voice of an exchange between close friends. He did not want Peter to act as a stumbling-block on the road which His Father chose for Him, and which He willingly followed. Without knowing it, Peter was playing the part of Satan, the great adversary and keeper of the "gates of hell", who had already tried to deflect Jesus from His saving mission when he tempted Him in the wilderness after His fast of forty days and nights, and who would continue his fiendish and jealous efforts to halt the Redemption. (cf *Mt* 4:1-11; 16:21-23)

The Condition for following Christ

Jesus did not want His Apostles' hearts to be troubled or afraid. He was strengthening their faith, and teaching them to understand His values and priorities. His love triumphs over sin, He redeems the world, and death becomes the gateway to life. "If anyone wants to be a follower of mine, let him renounce himself and take up his cross and follow me. For anyone who wants to save his life shall lose it, and anyone who loses his life for my sake will find it." He had first mentioned the cross when informing the newly-selected Apostles about the nature of their mission, and the need to renounce self. "Anyone who does not take his cross and follow in my footsteps is not worthy of me." The grim evidence of crucifixion was all too familiar to Galileans who witnessed the ruthless repression of any political rebellion. Jesus was no outlaw and His earlier hint at the manner of His death was too awful for them to contemplate but, as ever, in the most demanding circumstances He gives comfort in His paradox that anyone who loses his natural life for His sake will find an everlasting spiritual life, a truth which the Apostles gloriously prove. (*Mt* 10:38; 16:24-26).

The Inner Circle

From the Twelve Apostles whom Jesus appointed to share and continue His mission, Peter, James and John became an elite trio who were to be with Him on three occasions

The Foundation of the Church

which demonstrated the significance of unwavering faith in Christ. The first was when the twelve year old daughter of Jairus fell desperately ill. He was an elder of the synagogue at Capernaum who knew Jesus well and had witnessed His miracles. It was natural that he should go to Him for help, but even as he spoke word was brought that she had died. Jesus took Peter, James and John into the house where they saw Him restore the child to life. St Mark's account retains Our Lord's Aramaic "Tulitha Kumi" ("Little lamb, get up."), a phrase so indicative of gentle solicitude. Again He imposed silence on the witnesses of the miracle because the time had not come for the fulfilment of His command, "For there is nothing hidden but it must be disclosed, nothing kept secret except to be brought to light." (*Mk* 4:22; 5:35-43).

The Transfiguration

Six days after Peter's profession of faith at Caesarea Philippi, Jesus took him, with James and John, to Mount Tabor about two days walk away but familiar because it was only a few miles from Nazareth. On the heights, He revealed to them His glorious divinity which shone with the majesty of the Lord of Creation and Head of redeemed humanity. They saw Him talk to Moses and Elijah about what He had to accomplish in Jerusalem, the former dispensation of the law and the prophets united with the source of divine Truth who establishes a New Covenant between God and His people. Peter thought that such a wonder heralded a victorious Messianic reign, and that Moses and Elijah had come back to earth to enjoy the triumph. In his euphoria, he said it was a good thing that the three Apostles were on hand because from the trees at the summit they could improvise three shelters for Jesus and His visitors.

Moses, Elijah and Our Lord did not need earthly accommodation but Peter's considerate though impracticable suggestion elicited a further revelation about the Trinity. After Jesus' baptism by John in the Jordan, the Holy Spirit appeared as a dove, and the Father announced, "You are my Beloved Son in whom I am well pleased." Now, at this marvellous transfiguration on Tabor, the cloud of divine Presence enveloped the three Apostles, and they heard the Father's voice confirming what Peter had said at Caesarea Philippi. "This is my Beloved Son. Listen to all He says." The Father loves the Son whose words must be heeded, the Son loves the Father who wills redemption, and the Spirit who proceeds from their love reveals the Son who restores humanity to the Trinity. The vision passed and, once more, He was their familiar master and friend.

Our Lord's Transfiguration, the presence of Moses and Elijah, and the Father's declaration, illuminated everything He taught His Apostles about Himself and His relationship to the Old Law. The experience was to confirm their faith, prepare them for the trials of His

THE FOUNDATION OF THE CHURCH

forthcoming Passion and strengthen them to endure their own sufferings and eventual martyrdom. Again He told Peter, James and John to say nothing about what they had seen until after His Resurrection. He did not want their account to be misinterpreted, or inappropriate Messianic expectations to obscure the necessity of the Cross. From His royal throne, the all-powerful Word had descended from Heaven to take our human nature and give it immortal value. He had become one with man to reunite us to God and restore the gift of eternal life. At the start of His public life, He announced the mystery of the first regeneration in our own baptism. As the time of His suffering draws near, His Transfiguration is the mystery of the second regeneration, a share in His Resurrection through the Holy Spirit at work in the sacraments of His Body, the Church. It is a reminder that we pass through tribulation before entering God's Kingdom, but it is also the foretaste of Christ's glorious coming from Heaven which is our homeland. Then "He will transfigure these wretched bodies of ours into copies of His glorious body...by the same power with which He can subdue the universe." (*Mt* 17:1-9; *Mk* 9:2-10; *Lk* 9:28-36; *Ph* 3:21; *Ac* 14:22; *Catechism of the Catholic Church* 554). The third and final occasion is in twelve months time when Peter, James and John are with Jesus in the Garden of Gethsemane just before His arrest.

Jesus and Peter walk on the Sea of Galilee

When news was brought to Jesus that John the Baptist had been beheaded by order of Herod Antipas, He and the Apostles "withdrew by boat to a lonely place where they could be by themselves" to mourn their loss. As usual, He was to have no respite and, as soon as He stepped ashore, a large crowd was waiting. Although this was a moment of profound personal sadness, He made the needs of the people His priority. He healed the sick they had brought to Him and, before they returned home, gave them a meal by multiplying a few loaves and fishes, in a foretaste of the Eucharistic Banquet. He did not want the Apostles and Himself to be involved in the excitement which the miracle generated. He told them to go ahead by boat and He would follow as soon as He had sent the crowds home. They waited for Him some way off-shore but He slipped into the hills to pray quietly, so they set sail without Him.

A storm blew up and they were battling against a strong wind and a threatening sea when they saw a figure walking upon the waves towards them. At first, they thought it was a ghost but it was Jesus who called to them not to be afraid. Immediately, Peter wanted to be with Him and shouted, "Lord if it is you, tell me to come to you across the water." As soon as Jesus said "Come", he leapt out of the boat and set off over the surface, but the fierce wind and angry waves drained his confidence, and he began to sink. He shouted for help and Jesus stretched out His arms to save him, gently chiding his lack of faith. "It is me. Do not be afraid. Why did you doubt?" Both reached the safety of the boat, the storm abated, and all saluted Jesus as the Son of God whom the elements obey. When Matthew wrote his Gospel, Christ's followers were having a particularly hard time at the hands of some of the Jews, so the recollection of Peter's Barque giving refuge in life's stormy passages, and the Lord who calms the winds and the waves was particularly comforting.

Peter's faith wavered even though He could see the Lord, so it is not surprising if we who, for the moment, can see Him only with the eyes of faith, sometimes have doubts. Then we confidently pray "Lord I believe; help my unbelief." From the Father's belief in us we draw strength and our lives are fruitful. He works in us and helps us to appreciate and reciprocate that belief. Peter's attempt to cross the waters to Jesus is like our own passage to eternity at the end of life, the leap of faith into His loving arms expressed, for example, in the familiar 'Cwm Rhondda'

"When I tread the verge of Jordan bid my anxious fears subside;

Death of death and hell's destruction, land me safe on Canaan's side." (*W.Williams*)

In these last moments, Jesus comes to us across the water and holds out His hand. "Come", He says. "I am the Bread of Life." (cf. *Mt* 14: 13-33; *Mk* 4:35-41; 6:45-52).

Peter learns there are no limits to forgiveness

Peter's habit of asking blunt questions was a blessing in that they won answers from Jesus which say so much about the love of God for humanity, none more so than when he asked, "Lord, how often must I forgive my brother if he wrongs me? As much as seven times?" He assumed that there must be some kind of limit to forgiveness, and wanted to know at what precise point it was exhausted. Jesus told him he should forgive the offender "Seventy times seven". The Semitic preference for round and symbolic numbers is frequently seen in the Scriptures. Pharaoh, we remember, dreamed of seven fat and seven lean cattle, God told Moses that if Israel obeyed Him, He would put their enemies to flight in seven different ways, and the visionary of the Apocalypse saw the seven angels who brought the seven plagues which were the last of all because God's anger was exhausted. The number seven came to represent total perfection and sacred to the Jews who included a seven-branch candlestick in their religious observances.

The rabbis taught that it was sufficient to forgive an offence seven times, but Jesus maintained it did not matter if the number was seven, seventy-seven, or four hundred and ninety (7x70) because, in any case, one should lose count. He brought His Father's unlimited forgiveness and illustrated it with the parable of the heartless debtor as a reminder that "if a man has no pity, how can he plead for his own sins?" He had already taught Peter and the Apostles that they must be perfect in the manner of His heavenly Father, and ask Him to extend mercy to them in the measure that they pardon those who offend them. God's love is unconditional, absolute, enduring, and reveals itself by going to the farthest lengths in the sacrifice of His Son. "When the kindness and love of God our Saviour for mankind were revealed, it was not because He was concerned with any righteous actions we might have done ourselves; it was because of His own compassion that He saved us by means of the cleansing water of rebirth, and by renewing us with the Holy Spirit which He so generously poured over us through Jesus Christ our Saviour. He did this so that we should be justified by His grace to become heirs looking forward to inheriting eternal life." (cf. *Rv* 15:1-4; *Dt* 28:7; *Mt* 18:21-35; *Tt* 3:5-7).

HOLY THURSDAY

The Last Supper: Jesus washes the disciples' feet

Jesus longed to eat the Passover meal with His disciples because it was the prologue to the suffering and death which achieves our redemption and glorifies His Father. He wanted them to remember God's wonderful deeds of old, those of the present moment and those which, through Him and with their co-operation, are accomplished in ages yet to come. He sent Peter and John to hire an upper room with couches from one of the householders who rented accommodation to those who came to Jerusalem for the Feast. They made the necessary arrangements and it has been a pious, not unreasonable assumption that Peter did the catering. The Lamb of God who had demonstrated His love for mankind on so many occasions, was now about to give the Apostles the supreme proof of that love in His Sacrifice. Though conscious of His universal sovereignty and the incomparable dignity which had been seen in His Transfiguration, He rose from the table to perform the menial task of washing their feet, a service of deepest charity and a lesson in humility which far exceeded the ritual washing of hands. He went first to Peter who protested in horror at the thought of having his feet washed by the one whom he recognised as the Christ, the

HOLY THURSDAY

Son of the Living God. Even when asked to co-operate, he was adamant in a refusal which was born of love until Jesus told him that, unless He washed him, he would have no part in the Passion and its aftermath. Peter, aghast at the possibility of separation from his beloved Master, then went to the other extreme and asked to be washed all over.

Solemnly emphasising His relationship with the Father, Jesus informed the Apostles that no servant is greater than the master, no messenger greater than the sender and, if they behaved accordingly, they would experience the joy of true discipleship. Such a sublime moment gave way to the sad forecast of betrayal by one who shared His table, and whose treachery would rake His Sacred Heart. Judas knew of his own treachery but the rest, devastated that one of their close-knit group could deliver Jesus to His enemies, were fearfully bewildered about themselves and one another. For the moment, we must put aside da Vinci's familiar image of Jesus sitting at a western type table flanked by the Twelve, and picture a horse-shoe arrangement of cushions around a table just above ground level, with diners resting on one arm and reaching for food with the free hand. Typically, Peter wanted to end an intolerable situation and was near enough to John to whisper "Who is it?" John leaned towards Jesus with the familiarity of a bosom friend and asked Him, "Who is it Lord?" By way of answer, Jesus dipped a piece of bread in the oil and spice sauce and gave it to Judas who must have been reclining close to Him. It was a loving gesture but Judas' heart was already hardened by the devil, and he even tried to keep up appearances with "Not I Master, surely?" Jesus told him to do what he had to do without delay and, because exposure would have been unbearable, Judas immediately left the Light of the World and went into the night to meet the Prince of Darkness. (cf. *Mt* 26:25; *Jn* 13:1-15; 21-31).

Gethsemane

During the Paschal supper, Jesus renewed the promise made to Peter at the foundation of the Church: that the powers of darkness would never be victorious. "Simon, you must understand that Satan has got his wish to sift you like wheat, but I have prayed for you that your faith may not fail and, once you have recovered, you must strengthen your brethren."

"Lord," Peter replied. "I would be ready to go to prison with you, and to death", for while he was near Jesus, he could combat Satan with courage. His profession of selfless love was genuine, but it elicited the terrible prophecy from Jesus that before the second cock-crow heralded the dawn, he would deny his Master three times. The other Apostles were appalled but Jesus comforted them. "Let not your hearts be troubled." He was not going to leave them orphans, and would send the Paraclete to sustain and comfort them. They must realise, however, that human frailty can stifle fervour and, when He foretold Peter's denial, it was a reminder us that He knows us better than we know ourselves. Saint Philip Neri's prayer acknowledges that the way to defeat Satan is to keep close to the Fountain of Grace, "Lord, keep your hand on Philip, or Philip will betray you."

The Passover meal of the Old Covenant celebrated the love and mercy of the Father-God who delivered His chosen people from Egyptian slavery in anticipation of the redemption from sin achieved by the Son. It recalled the sacrifice of the spotless lamb eaten with unleavened bread, and its blood sprinkled on the doorposts so that the avenging angel would "pass over" their homes and they would be protected from the destroying plague. In family communion with His Apostles, the Lamb of God establishes the Eternal Covenant and institutes the sacrament of the Holy Eucharist. In a new, sublime Passover He rids humanity of the bonds of sin and, with His blood, restores it to life with God. (cf *Lk* 22:7-13; *Ex* 12:1-8; 11-14).

They left the supper-room in the north-west quarter of Jerusalem, and went out of the city by the Water Gate near the Pool of Siloe. Turning north past the Temple esplanade outside Solomon's Porch, they crossed the Brook Kedron ("turbid water-stream") to enter the garden estate of Gethsemane ("olive-press"). This was on the western slope of Mount Olivet near Bethany where Martha, Mary and Lazarus lived, and probably belonged to another friend. It was one of Jesus' favourite retreats, and Judas knew he could find Him there when he brought the arresting party of soldiers, Levitical priests and servants of the chief priests. Jesus began to dread what was in store, and He took Peter, James and John some little distance from the others so that they could keep supportive watch while He prayed to His Father. His hour of suffering had come and human nature recoiled from the prospect of the pain and fearsome burden of sin which He must shoulder and expiate with His death. He was racked with anguish not only at the prospect of crucifixion, but by Israel's incredulity and callous rejection, the inconstancy of His closest friends, and mankind's ingratitude.

God the Son submitted Himself to the Father's will but, in His agony, beads of perspiration became drops of blood, a phenomenon occasioned by intense fear and mental torment. Distressed, He paced back and forth three times, needing companiable comfort but, despite earlier protestations of reliability, Peter, James and John were asleep. With disappointment and isolation came calm resignation, and His reproach, directed to Peter was gentle. "Could you not have watched just an hour with me?" Even the elite trio had forgotten everything He had said about the need to be watchful, and that fine words and good intentions must be sustained by vigilant prayer so that the devil's temptations are overcome, and steadfast loyalty to Christ maintained in every tribulation.

It was a lesson Peter came to appreciate and share. "Be calm but vigilant because your enemy, the devil, is prowling around like a roaring lion looking for someone to eat...Stand up to him, strong in faith...You will have to suffer only for a little while; the God of all grace who called you to eternal glory in Christ will see that all is well again." (cf. *Mt* 26:36-56; *Mk* 13:33-37; 14:32-42; *Lk* 22:31-46; *Jn* 15-19; *1 P* 5:8-11).

Jesus is arrested

While Jesus was with them the Apostles were stout-hearted, especially Peter. When Judas arrived with the armed guard to arrest Jesus, he drew his sword and cut off the ear of Malchus, a servant of the high-priest. Despite the odds, he was so obviously ready for a fight that Jesus had to tell him to sheath his sword. It is surprising that he was not arrested on the spot and was no doubt saved when Jesus' intervened and miraculously reunited the servant with his severed ear. However, as soon as Jesus was led captive to the high priest's palace, the Apostles fled for their lives, though Peter followed at a distance, keeping his Master in sight. He managed to enter the courtyard, perhaps with the help of John who was known as an acquaintance of the high-priest. He tried to avoid detection by mingling with those waiting to see what was happening and keeping warm at the braziers on a chilly night, but one of the servants heard him speaking and recognised his voice. Three times he was asked if he was a disciple and friend of the Prisoner, and three times he vehemently denied any association with the one whom he had been the first to hail as "the Christ, the Son of the Living God." As Jesus was being taken across the courtyard to the guard-house, He heard Peter. He turned and looked at him stretching out his hands to the glowing coals; their eyes met and Peter's heart broke. It is said that when he died, his cheeks were deeply furrowed by the tears of repentance which he shed.

The Resurrection and the Shepherd of the Flock

It was the Sabbath Eve when Jesus was taken down from the Cross and laid in the sepulchre, so Joseph of Arimathea was not able to embalm His body. Early on the Sunday, when Mary Magdalen went ahead of the other women who were going to perform this last service for the Lord, she found the stone rolled back from the entrance, and the sepulchre empty. She ran to tell Peter and John who raced to the tomb, the latter outstripping his senior. He peered through the opening and saw the linen cloths lying on the ground but did not go in, waiting respectfully for Peter who entered as soon as he arrived. He was amazed at what he saw. The burial bandages were not in a confused heap but lay where the body had been, and the napkin which had covered the head was neatly rolled. This eliminated any body-snatching theory, for such thieves do not carefully remove linen bands before making off with their booty. When John entered, the light of faith enabled him to see at once the truth of the Scriptures that Christ would rise from the dead.

On Sunday evening, the Apostles were still taking refuge in the room they had rented the previous Thursday. Their Master had met a horrifying death at the hands of the religious authorities who might now direct their hatred towards His followers. They knew about the rumours in Jerusalem that they had stolen Jesus' body, and feared for their own lives. Then Mary Magdalen told them of her meeting with Jesus whom she had initially mistaken for the gardener. The women who went to embalm Jesus' body, had been instructed by an angel to inform the disciples, especially Peter, that the Lord was risen, and later He appeared to Peter himself. Two disciples, Cleophas and, some say, Luke who had set off for their home village of Emmaus about six miles west of Jerusalem to cope with their grief and disappointment, had rushed back with news that Jesus had met them on their journey, walked with them as far as the village, shared their supper and revealed Himself to them in the breaking of bread. With mounting happiness and excitement, however, came the suspicion that some news was too good to be true, and Peter and the Apostles (Thomas was elsewhere) remained behind closed doors.

Suddenly, Jesus was with them, His glorified Body needing no open door. He greeted them with His peace and showed the wounds of His hands and side to prove His identity. He asked them for something to eat to show He was no ghost and ate the grilled fish they offered. He told them that just as the Father had sent Him, now he was sending them with authority to continue His mission of salvation. Just as God breathed life into Adam at the Creation, the Risen Lord, through whom all things are made, now breathed on the Apostles to communicate to them the Holy Spirit in anticipation of the gifts they would receive at Pentecost. He ordained them to forgive sins on His behalf and, on this most glorious day in history, instituted the Sacrament of Reconciliation, a powerful sign of the Peace He brings and which the world cannot give. He visited them again a week later when Thomas was there, and the Apostle famous for his doubts recognised and acclaimed Jesus' divinity with immediate adoration, "My Lord and my God."

Peter was the first Apostle to whom Jesus appeared after His Resurrection because He wanted to reassure him that his sorrow for the denial in the courtyard of the high priest's palace had brought forgiveness, and that their relationship was unaffected. It was also to strengthen the faith of the others who were able to say, "the Lord has indeed risen and has appeared to Simon." Peter is particularly involved in the dawn of the new creation which began on the first Easter morning and, as the prime witness to Christ's victory over death, he leads the

Apostles who are the foundation stones of the Church. (cf. *Mk* 16:8; *Lk* 22:31-32; 24:12-36, 43; *Jn* 14:17; 20:1-9, 21; *Catechism of the Catholic Church* 640-42).

After His memorable appearances to the Apostles on the first Easter Sunday and the Paschal Octave, they felt confident that circumstances in Jerusalem no longer posed a threat to Him, so they returned to Galilee where most of them had homes. One morning Peter, James, John, Nathanael, Thomas and at least two others who had returned to the fisherman's life, were approaching their moorings at Capernaum after another luckless night. They spotted a figure on the shore about a hundred yards away but could not distinguish who it was, either because of the early morning mist or because, for the moment, Jesus chose to remain unrecognised. He called to them in a manner which speaks volumes about the warm comradeship He shared with His followers. "Boys", He shouted, "have you caught anything to eat?" (cf. Latin Vulgate's "pueri", "lads/boys"). They were in no mood for jolly exchanges and, no doubt irritated and embarrassed by their failure, answered a surly "No".

The Figure urged the unsuccessful crew to try again on the starboard side. The vessel was heading south close to the western shore, so this was the least likely place to find fish. Maybe memories of an earlier miraculous draught began to stir but, whatever the reason, it does them credit that they dropped the nets for a catch. The result was a magnificent haul of one hundred and fifty-three fish. Saint Jerome (340-425) draws attention to the importance of this detail because the ancient world believed it to be the exact number of all known species of fish. It was an indication of the universality of God's love, and of the Church which embraces a new people from every corner of the globe. John who recognised Jesus first said, "It is the Lord", but it was Peter who leapt into the water to reach Him as quickly as possible. When they came on shore, Jesus cooked them breakfast to assure them that He was no apparition but was physically present, again in the breaking of bread.

After they had eaten, Jesus asked Peter three times if he loved Him. Peter's final answer was touching in its sadness at having to be asked three times. "Lord, you know everything; you know that I love you." The triple denial was expiated and repentance was complete. The Good Shepherd whose love is beyond the power of human expression, confirmed Peter as chief of the Apostles and three times He delegated the often hazardous responsibility of caring for His Flock: "Feed my lambs...Look after my sheep...Feed my sheep." Peter's appointment and commission are inherited by his successors who are the Popes and Christ's vicars on earth and the pastoral office, with royal authority and responsibility, is at the heart of the Church and is perpetuated by the bishops under the primacy of the Pope. (cf. *Lk* 22:31-34; *Jn* 21:1-19; *Catechism of the Catholic Church* 881).

The Ascension

Peter and the ten Apostles who remained after Judas had hanged himself in a fit of despair, resolutely stayed in Jerusalem until the end of Paschal week but, as we know, returned to their homes and occupations once they were sure Jesus was in no danger. During the next five weeks, He appeared regularly to these closest followers and reminded them about the Kingdom of God. He told them that when He was gone they were to return to Jerusalem and wait there until the Holy Spirit came to baptise them as the Father promised. According to Saint Matthew, He arranged to meet them on the high ground above the Sea of Galilee which, some say, was the site of the Sermon on the Mount and, if so, was splendidly appropriate. Saint Luke says that Jesus ascended from the outskirts of Bethany, the village beside Mount Olivet, and repeats this in the early lines of the Acts of the Apostles, but the difference of opinion may arise from his condensed account of events after the Resurrection.

The Apostles were desolate at the thought of Jesus' departure. Despite everything He had taught them, we know from the disappointment of the two disciples going to Emmaus that hopes for an immediate Messianic reign in Israel with, perhaps, suitable positions for themselves had not entirely vanished. Patiently He explained that after His return to the Father He would, within ten days, send the Holy Spirit, the Paraclete and Advocate, to stay with them, teach them and remind them of everything He had said, and inspire humanity's progress to eternal life. They would be empowered to represent Him not only in Jerusalem, Judaea and Samaria but throughout the whole world.

In the ultimate assurance of his divinity, Jesus told the Apostles that He had total authority over Heaven and earth. He commanded them, therefore, to go and enable all nations to become His disciples, and baptise them in the name of the Trinity to which He, the Person of the Incarnate God, was about to return. In this "Great Commission" and mandate for evangelisation, they were to teach everyone to observe the precepts He had given them. This was no easy task, but His light and the strength of His presence would be with them and their successors until the end of time. From the high ground, Our Lord then ascended into Heaven and was lost to the Apostles' sight, but two angels came to comfort them and all His followers throughout the ages. "Jesus who has been taken from you...will come back the same way as you have seen Him go," when He will return in glory on the clouds of Heaven accompanied by His angels who will serve His judgement. Peter and the Apostles became and remain the supreme exemplars of evangelisation, their achievements the more remarkable and heaven-blessed in that they did not see the results of their efforts and the fulfilment of Christ's promises, or enjoy the riches of two thousand years of Christian Faith. (cf. *Mt* 24:30-31; 28:16-20; *Lk* 24:18-24, 49; *Ac* 1:1-14).

THE PRIMACY OF PETER

The Election of Matthias

After the Ascension, the Apostles and other disciples followed Jesus' instructions and returned to Jerusalem where it seems they stayed in the house of Saint Mark's mother (cf. *Ac* 12:12). While they waited for the Holy Spirit, they were united in prayer with Mary, the Mother of Jesus, whose last mention in the Scriptures is her significant presence at the birth of her Son's Church. Peter's leadership and belief in God's word quickly became apparent as he addressed the disciples who had gathered in Jerusalem, and invited nominations to fill the vacancy in the Apostolic College left by Judas. He made no attempt to impose his own choice but the power which Jesus had conferred on him was already active, and he took the opportunity to establish the qualifications required for Apostleship. It was essential for an Apostle to have been a follower of Jesus from the time of His baptism by John right through to His Ascension, and be able to testify to the truth of the Resurrection. When discussion identified two candidates of equal merit, Peter felt that the choice should be left not to human nature but to the Lord Himself who had personally appointed the other Apostles. Because the Holy Spirit had not yet come to invest him with full authority, he led the infant Church community in the first recorded prayer to Christ, not in expectation of divine intervention but as an expression of obedience to His guiding providence. Lots were drawn and Matthias was elected. This method was not uncommon in Jewish religious society and was used, for example to distribute the Temple's sacerdotal offices, as when Zechariah, John the Baptist's father, won the prized and sacred task of offering incense in the Holy of Holies.

Pentecost

The Festival of Pentecost was celebrated on the fiftieth day after Passover to give thanks for the harvest and for the Law which God gave to Moses on Sinai. It is now associated with the Birthday of the Christian Church. The community was still together when the Holy Spirit came from Heaven in the form of a powerful wind which would disperse the disciples on their world-wide mission. God showed His enabling presence in tongues of fire, first united, and then separate to rest on each one whom Jesus had promised would teach and baptise the scattered nations with fire and the Holy Spirit. They were endowed with His gifts, including the ability to transcend language differences. They communicated with every visitor to Jerusalem for the Festival, as well as the residents, and everyone understood what they were saying about the marvels of God. The Gospel was reaching out to people of every nation, and a new spiritual language was being learnt by the whole world as the Holy Spirit breathed life into the Church, the community of the new and universal Kingdom.

Peter's address to the assembly

Before His Ascension, Jesus reminded the Apostles of His teachings. What was written in the Psalms, the Law, and the Prophets about His suffering, death and Resurrection was to be fulfilled and, in His name, they were to preach repentance for the forgiveness of sins to the world. Peter, once so frightened that he had denied Jesus, was particularly inspired and his remarkable transformation was evidence of the promised power of the Resurrection and the gifts of the Holy Spirit. In a fearless, authoritative speech he first reproached his listeners for doing nothing to prevent Jesus' death, and then consoled them with the message that God, who had raised Him back to life, now called them to Himself with all their sins forgiven. On this Feast of the Old Law, he interpreted the prophecies and introduced a New Law which was for the benefit of all nations. The subjects of this inaugural Christian Sermon became the standard for the early Church: Jesus was the promised Messiah whom the religious leaders had not recognised. Unjustly, they had put him to death but, after three days, He rose again from the dead as He had foretold and, in so doing, He had conquered death and won salvation for all who believe in Him.

Tactfully, Peter explained why everyone, irrespective of native language, had been able to understand the disciples. The miracle of communication presented the Risen Jesus as the Messiah who welcomed all without exception to His Kingdom, and the chief Apostle spoke with such conviction that the crowd accepted what he said, with the dramatic result that three thousand were baptised. With John's assistance, he competently defended the Apostle's position and doctrine of the Resurrection before the aristocratic Sanhedrin who were amazed at the assurance of laymen whom they thought ignorant. True, they were not expert in rabbinical methodology but the guidance of the Holy Spirit and, above all, the influence of personal association with Jesus more than compensated for human inadequacy. (cf. *Ex* 3:2; *Mal* 3:2-3; *Ps* 16; *Lk* 3:16; 12:49-50; 24:44-49; *Jn* 14:26; 16:7-14; *Ac* 2:1-42; 4-13)

This startling success engendered a sense of community which expressed itself in a readiness to share money and possessions in a new pattern of life. Those with goods and property sold them, and Peter organised the Apostles to distribute the proceeds. The willingness to share all things in common was partly prompted by the expectation that it would not be long before Jesus returned from Heaven, but it did re-distribute wealth which had been concentrated in a small proportion of the population. Not all were honest in generosity, however, and Peter had to deal purposefully with Ananias and his wife Sapphira who secretly retained some of the money from the sale of their property. Nor was distribution always equitable, and the Greek speaking community, admittedly better off than their Jewish counterparts, complained when their widows did not receive a fair share. The disposal of property, admirable in so many ways, later caused some hardship for the infant Church in Jerusalem during the Empire-wide famine of 46-7 AD.

Peter's primacy in the mother-church in Jerusalem was characterised by apostolic zeal, a rich liturgical prayer life in the Temple and private houses, and miraculous cures. Loyalty to the Temple and fidelity to Jewish customs preserved the important relationship with Judaeism. Disagreements over the care of widows and the interpretation of dietary regulations were short-lived, and the truth of Jesus' parables about the Kingdom became evident: the smallest seed growing to a mustard tree with enough branches to house every kind of bird; a tiny amount of yeast generating a vast quantity of dough. Compared to earlier faint-heartedness, the vibrant courage of the Apostles determined to stay in Jerusalem where Jesus had been executed, owed much to Peter's example. Hostile elements in the city could not halt expansion, and the number of disciples grew so quickly that the decision was made to appoint deacons to help with social administration so that the Apostles could concentrate on teaching and the prayer-life which supports it. Seven, the perfect number, were chosen, all of whom had Greek names, and one was Stephen who was to be the first martyr. Admittedly, Some disciples moved to less menacing areas, but this brought the Gospel to people like the Samaritans, hitherto ostracised for being of mixed blood, and the Apostles were quick to exploit the potential of organised missions beyond Jerusalem.

Peter's vision

As soon as the Church in Judaea, Galilee and Samaria entered a period of relative calm, Peter was able to visit other Christian groups who had fled from Jerusalem to escape Saul's persecution. At Lydda, on Palestine's fertile coastal plain, he cured a paralytic called Aeneas, and this encouraged an appeal from disciples in Joppa, twelve miles to the north, where a much loved woman called Tabitha had just died. He went immediately and brought her back to life. He lodged in the house of Simon who as a tanner followed an occupation which was particularly disparaged by the Jews. Contact with animal hide made a person ritually unclean and it was the rabbinical opinion that "the world cannot exist without tanners but woe unto him who is a tanner." Many of Jesus' followers still thought His revelation was uniquely for the Jews, and Peter was not yet accustomed to seeing himself as a missionary. However, his choice of

THE PRIMACY OF PETER

accommodation was an indication of his awareness that a wider world waited to receive the Gospel.

One day, he went on to the flat roof of Simon's house to say mid-day prayer. He had not eaten, was probably suffering from overwork, and the sun beat down on him. As he prayed, he fell into a kind of trance and in the sky saw a great movement of a sheet containing every kind of fowl and reptile being lowered by ropes. He heard a voice which shouted, "Get up Peter; kill and eat." Among the creatures were some which the Mosaic law forbade Jews to eat and demanded they keep their distance from those who did. "Not so Lord," Peter answered, "for I have never eaten anything that is common or unclean." The Voice replied, "Do not call common that which God has made clean." The vision faded and Peter came to his senses. He was thinking about the vision when he heard three foreign voices at Simon's door in the street below. He went down and asked the callers, one of whom was a soldier, if he could be of help. They said they came from Cornelius, the centurion at Caesarea, who asked Peter to visit him. He was one of the Roman officers stationed in Palestine of whom the New Testament speaks well. He could not have been fully aware of the Resurrection, but he worshipped God devoutly, supported the Jewish faith, and God had sent an angel to tell him to contact Peter.

The vision's meaning became clear. In a powerful and respected foreigner, God had awakened an interest in

Jesus, and Peter began to appreciate that the food laws should be relaxed. He was cautious about new ideas but understood that the Gentiles were part of God's Kingdom and should be welcomed into the Church on equal terms, so he went to Caesarea and took six of the Joppa community with him to witness events. Cornelius was waiting at home with his family and household. Although it was forbidden for a Jew to enter an alien house, Peter did not hesitate for he knew that God makes no distinction between persons. The Paraclete was at work in a new Pentecost, and he and his companions felt the transforming effect of the Holy Spirit's powerful presence. Peter announced that he brought news of the Resurrection and the forgiveness of sin to all people, including the Gentiles. and baptised Cornelius and his household into the community

When he returned to Jerusalem he was criticised for associating with Gentiles, for eating with them and, in what seemed the most serious contravention of Mosaic Law, admitting them to Church membership without benefit of circumcision. When Peter told them about the vision in Joppa and its aftermath, they accepted the evidence of God's will and approved his action. A movement once preoccupied with Judaeism was emerging as the Universal Church and, as new districts were evangelised, Peter assumed full pastoral powers and responsibilities. (cf. *Lv* 11; *Mk* 8:5-13; *Ac* 8-11)

THE PRIMACY OF PETER

Peter imprisoned

Herod Agrippa courted popularity not only with Rome but also with his Jewish subjects by persecuting Jesus' followers, especially the Apostles who had attracted adverse public opinion by welcoming Gentiles. He levelled a false political charge against James, the brother of John, and had him beheaded. This so pleased the Jews that he threw Peter into prison for good measure, but "the Church prayed to God for him unremittingly" and he escaped through the good offices of an angel sent by God. The Key of David who released Israel from Egyptian captivity, unlocks Peter's prison chains, and liberates us from the slavery of sin. By His sacrifice He "purifies us so that we become His very own" and opens the gates of the everlasting Kingdom. While attending games in thanksgiving for Claudius' safe return from his expedition to Britain, Herod was seized with a violent gastric attack, and died in agony. (cf. *Ac* 12; *Tt* 2:11-14)

Peter in Rome

The later chapters of the Acts concentrate more on Saint Paul's apostolate to the wider Gentile world than on Peter's supportive leadership and mission in Asia Minor before he went to Rome. That his noble work for his Master ended there is confirmed by Clement, Ignatius and Irenaeus who testify to the establishment of the Church and its hierarchical tradition in the city. The titles "first pope" and "Bishop of Rome" describe Peter's unique vocation but it was not until the pontificate of Pius I in 142 AD that the single bishop system of hierarchy was identified.

Peter's Letters

The migration of the Jews from their homeland began with the Assyrian invasion around 720 BC, increased through the Babylonian Exile, and continued after the Roman conquest and subsequent destruction of the Temple. They settled principally in Babylon, Egypt, around the shores of the Mediterranean, and eastward to Mesopotamia, so that in New Testament times there were as many living outside Palestine as within it. Significantly, the letter of James (1:1), for example, is addressed to the "Twelve Tribes of the Dispersion" who stayed true to their motherland, making pilgrimage to the great festivals and paying the Temple taxes.

It was in the early days of Nero's persecution that Peter wrote his two letters from Rome which he refers to as "Babylon". (*1 Peter* 5:3). He says how much he valued the support and friendship of (John) Mark the evangelist, and Silvanus (Silas) who had been at Antioch with Paul and Barnabas, and had accompanied Paul on his second mission in Asia Minor. The Christians in the Roman provinces knew the sufferings experienced by their brethren in the capital and Peter wrote to comfort them, and give them hope and encouragement so that they should not waver themselves. He urged those already victimised for following Christ, and slandered as criminals and slaves, to remember that suffering should come as no surprise in the light of what Christ had to endure, that it had much to teach, and should never be an excuse for unacceptable behaviour.

The letters are assured, compassionate and timeless in their relevance. They are addressed to all deprived of legal status and security, who feel estranged from the attitudes and values around them, and who are the victims of hostility. He asks them to remain firm in their faith, and rejoice that their lives have been transformed to a new birth as a chosen race, a royal priesthood, the people of God who are heirs to the Kingdom of Heaven. As individuals and communities, their lives must carry the signs of holiness, with deeds speaking louder than words and in relationships characterised by mutual respect and gentleness. Great care should be taken to avoid the influence of false teachers who claim that there will be no Second Coming, no judgement by God, and that fulfilment is to be attained in this earthly life. As his own neared its conclusion, Peter gave the world his final exhortation to be true to the faith and watch for the day when Jesus returns in glory.

Jesus had foretold the kind of death which Peter would undergo. "I tell you most solemnly, when you were young you put on your own belt and walked where you liked. But when you grow old you will stretch out your hands and somebody else will put a belt around you and take you where you would rather not go. Follow me." (*Jn* 21:19). In his crucifixion he did, indeed, follow His Master with hands and arms outstretched. The signs are that he was buried in the pagan graveyard situated on the Vatican Hill. In 160 AD, approximately the centenary of his death, Pope St Anicetus (155-66), installed a 'Tropaion', a victory monument, in a brick wall over one of the graves. In 325 AD, Constantine built a basilica there, following the custom of erecting a place of worship where the bodies of the saints were believed to rest. He had prepared the foundations five years earlier by filling the cemetary with compacted soil and rubble. Because Roman Law forbade such violation of a graveyard, this imperial exercise of flexibility gives weight to the conviction that this was Peter's resting place.

When the warrior Julius II became Pope in 1503, he instructed Bramante to draw up plans for a new basilica to replace the Constantine original, and he laid the foundation stone in 1506. For a variety of political reasons, there was little progress until Pope Paul III (1534-49), best remembered for convening the Council of Trent, engaged Michelangelo to supervise the building which was virtually completed when the artist died in 1564. Thirty years later, when Pope Clement VIII finalised the position of the present high altar, he deliberately placed it directly above those which had earlier been erected by Popes Callistus II in 1127, and St Gregory the Great in 594.

In 1939, Pope Pius XII initiated preparations for his predecessor, Pius XI, to be interred beside the tomb of St Pius X in the crypt of St Peter's Basilica. Opportunity was taken to lower its floor so as to give reasonable height to an additional place of worship, and the accompanying excavations revealed the floor of Constantine's basilica, beneath which lay a line of Roman tombs. On the wall of one was the inscription "Peter, pray Christ Jesus for the holy Christian men buried near your body", an invocation similar to those expressed in graffiti in the Catacombs. Continued excavation disclosed the Tropaion which Anicetus had erected, and to the right of this was found a marble-lined repository in which lay bones which scientific study showed to be those of a stocky man in his sixties. These had been shrouded in a cloth of imperial purple and gold, a sign of the great veneration in which the deceased and his status were held. On June 27th 1968, Pope Paul VI declared the relics to be those of the Prince of the Apostles. He conducted them back to the repository in the crypt of Saint Peter's Basilica which rests upon the Rock chosen by Christ to be the foundation of His Church.

The Petrine Succession and Heritage

Prior to calling His disciples, Jesus said "Repent for the Kingdom of Heaven is close at hand." It is the Kingdom of justice, love and peace in all their fullness as Creation sings the praises of God, and for the coming of which He taught them to pray in the "Our Father".

The Church, this Kingdom on earth instituted by God the Son can be identified by the chain of authority which links Peter, the Apostles and their mission to the bishops today. With the Pope as the well-spring of unity in the Apostolic Church, the teaching of the Gospel is treasured and disseminated so that all may know the universal nature of God's love. In the Petrine Succession, the Bishops of Rome follow Peter as his vicars and temporal leaders of the all-embracing Church. Peter, who with Paul founded the Apostolic See of Rome, does not have a literal successor because only he and the Apostles are able to testify that the Risen Christ is the Jesus who told them that they would be with Him on Judgement day. "I confer a Kingdom on you...You will eat and drink at my table in my Kingdom and you will sit on thrones to judge the twelve tribes of Israel." However, Peter does have heirs to perpetuate his commission to evangelise the world, in communion with all the baptised. When Jesus gave him the keys of the Kingdom, he received them on behalf of the Church, and the essential nature of collegiate responsibility shared with the Apostles is perpetuated in the authoritative relationship of the Pope with the bishops. He told him to confirm the faith of his brethren, and the Apostles that the leaders among them must become as the one who serves. The spiritual power of Peter's successors, therefore, remains one of service and is the bond which unites the Church to the New Testament. (*Mt* 4:17; *Lk* 22:33)

Ut Unum Sint

"May they all be one. Father may they be one in us as you are in me and I am in you, so that the world may believe it was you who sent me." (*Jn* 17:21). Our Lord's words in His concluding prayer at the Last Supper are the inspiration for Pope John Paul II's Encyclical Letter *'Ut Unum Sint'* ('May they be one'), 1995, a contribution to achieving the "noble goal of the full communion of all Christians." He writes "to encourage the efforts of all who work for the cause of unity which is a specific duty of the Bishop of Rome" and reflects that Our Lord has given a ministry to the successor of the Apostle Peter to support a communion of Churches in authentic unity of faith, charity, mission, and the sacraments.

Since the Second Vatican council, the Church has seen the Papacy undertaking a wider role, not least by way of the Pope's worldwide apostolic journeys, his fearless pronouncements, and the quality of his prolific writings. "The primacy of the Bishop of Rome… now appears as an essential theme in the theological dialogue between the Catholic Church and other Churches, and in the ecumenical movement as a whole... so that ecclesial communities are taking a fresh look at the ministry of unity." (cf. *'Ut Unum Sint'*, 96.)

The Apostles' Creed

According to tradition, the Apostles composed a summary of Christian belief based on their personal experience of seeing and hearing what Jesus did and said. The Creed's theological foundation is traced to the first decades of the Church's life and encapsulates the Apostles' thinking and intentions. Today, many ecumenical discussions end with the expressed hope that the Apostles' Creed should be regarded as the universal expression of Christian Faith in short clauses or "articles". God the Father and the work of Creation is the subject of the first article; 2-7 make particular mention of God the Son and the work of Redemption; 8-12 teach of God the Holy Spirit and the work of Sanctification.

(1)"I believe in God the Father Almighty, Creator of heaven and earth. (2)And in Jesus Christ, His only Son our Lord (3) who was conceived by the Holy Spirit, born of the Virgin Mary, (4)suffered under Pontius Pilate, was crucified, died and was buried; He descended into hell; (5) the third day He rose again from the dead; (6) He ascended into Heaven and is seated at the right hand of God the Father Almighty; (7) from thence he shall come to judge the living and the dead. (8) I believe in the Holy Spirit, (9) the holy Catholic Church, the communion of saints, (10) the forgiveness of sins, (11) the resurrection of the body, (12) and life everlasting."

The Didache

The number of Apostles was not random and, after Judas' death, the election of Matthias restored the membership to twelve who witnessed the life, death and resurrection of Jesus upon which the Faith is based, and who transmit His teachings. "The Didache", or "The Teaching of the Lord to the Gentiles through the Twelve Apostles", is a first century book of basic instructions for Christians based on early sources and traditions:

Chapters 1-6, 'The Two Ways', incorporate Matthew's record of the Sermon on the Mount, excerpts from the Qumran 'Manual of Discipline', 'The Letter of Barnabas', and 'Doctrina Apostolorum', (the teaching of the Apostles), about how Jewish heritage influenced the development of early Christianity. The Apostles emerge as "the rulers" guided by the Holy Spirit whom Jesus promised would teach them all things and convince them of sin, justice and judgement. Consequently, their decisions are His decisions, and whoever lies to them lies to the Holy Spirit whom God gives to the baptised.

Chapters 7-10 are liturgical instructions.

Chapters 11-15 are the disciplinary regulations concerning bishops, deacons, divisions in communities, and the Holy Eucharist.

The Didache concludes with an exhortation to be on the watch for the Anti-Christ, and to remain faithful until the Second Coming of the Lord.

Apostolic Succession

The principle of succession is the continuation, through the bishops, of the duty of pastoral care which Jesus entrusted to the Apostles. Because their mission lasts to the end of time, arrangements were made to appoint successors so that the Flock, which is the Church, would always be tended. Peter's individual responsibility passes to bishops whose pre-eminence lies in their association with the Apostles through continuous succession. (cf. *Matthew* 28:20; *Luke* 10:16ff; *Dogmatic Constitution on the Church*, n.20ff).

In their lifetime, the Apostles shared their ministry with others so that the needs of the faithful should be met. Distinguished examples include Paul, Luke, Mark, missionaries like Barnabas and Timothy who helped found new churches, and the resident local leaders who extended the Apostles' role to teach, baptise, forgive sin and look after successive generations. (cf. *Acts* 20:18-35; *2 Timothy* 2:2; 4:1-8). With these co-workers, the Apostles established collegiate leadership in the churches where the elders presided and taught in the community. Pope Clement I, whose letter to the Corinthians is the most important first century document outside the New Testament, says that the system was working well by 100AD, that the first generation had been appointed by the Apostles themselves, and the second by "other eminent men" according to the rules they had laid down for the appointment of their successors in the ministry.

Ignatius of Antioch (35-107AD) says that, first in the east and then in the west, a single episcopacy evolved from the collegiate local system with one bishop in charge. Second century Christian writings refer to the belief that these bishops were the successors of the Apostles and guardians of their tradition. This was verified by Irenaeus (130-200) in his treatise 'Against the (Gnostic) Heretics', and by Tertullian (160-225AD) who drew attention to the teaching role of successive bishops as they led churches to witness the apostolic "rule of faith". Hippolytus (170-236AD) described how neighbouring bishops ordained a new bishop for his church, an indication that a share in the apostolic mandate was received and given through ordination by those who already possessed it. He recorded the ordination prayer which expresses the belief that bishops participate in the authority which Christ delegated to the Apostles, and that the Holy Spirit endows them with all gifts necessary for their ministry.

ACKNOWLEDGEMENTS

The CTS gratefully acknowledges use of prayers, scripture quotations and hymns from:

The Jerusalem Bible, Darton, Longman & Todd, London, 1974.
Catechism of the Catholic Church, Geoffrey Chapman, London 1994.
The Divine Office, Collins, London, 1974.
Papal Documents, Catholic Truth Society, London.
Westminster Hymnal, Burns, Oates & Washbourne, London, 1948.

Bibliography

Catholic Commentary on the Holy Scripture, Thomas Nelson & Sons, London, 1951.
The Tomb of St Peter, M. Guarducci, Harrap, London, 1960.
The Bones of St Peter, M. Walsh, Victor Gollanz, London, 1983.
Cambridge Companion to the Bible, Cambridge University Press 1997.
A History of Christianity, Owen Chadwick, Weidenfeld & Nicholson, London, 1995
The Papacy, Paul Johnson, Weidenfeld & Nicholson, London, 1997.
The Story of Christianity, M. Collins & M. Price, Dorling Kindersley, London, 1999.
Commentary on the Whole Bible, Matthew Henry, Harper Collins, London, 1960.